Invest

IN YOUR HOME

JOAN MARIE

Contents

After reading all the bad news about black homeownership I decided to write a book. I have a real-estate license along with over 20 years of property development/management under my belt I would like to mention. So when I say I decided to a write a book, it is not on a whim. I have been employed in this area for a very long time.

Yes it is true that property in black neighborhoods across the United States don't go up in value like in white neighborhoods. It is also true that many black people are not homeowners because of economic reasons and discrimination, etc… But what I want to focus on is how we as black people can increase the value of our properties in our neighborhoods.

I live in a predominately black community and really I wouldn't have it any other way. I like being around my own people, its only natural. I feel comfortable around black people like myself and I don't see anything wrong with that. I have heard so many black people say they want to live in white communities because their houses keep their value and even increase in value faster than in black communities, which is true. However, did you know that many stats show that if a community have a black population of 10% or more then that community value will increase slower. I think that the solution is not to move out of our communities, I think we need to stay in our communities and make them better. We need to better our school systems so that we won't have to pay for our children to go to catholic schools or private schools in order to get an education because the public schools in our areas are poorly ran.

I am saying we need to start putting and keeping our tax dollars in our own communities to build them up. This is not new information for you. You have heard it before and seen it in other groups that live right here in the United States. They settle in their own communities and participate in their community governments and school systems all the time. It doesn't take a rocket scientist to figure this out does it? NO! So what are waiting for?

It really bothers me that our community property values are less I mean, way less than that of white communities. Some will tell you its all about location. Well after my observation, we can live in the most convenient locations and still our property values will be much lower than our white counter parts. So really what is it? Well I think it is many different reasons but, I want to just talk about the reasons, I think are really affecting our property values as black homeowners.

I think that if we could just do the things I am going to discuss in this little book, we could actually increase property values in our communities across the country. Now I know some of you may say well, no it's more than that. We can't find jobs, or most of us are single parents etc… And you are right. However, I still believe we can increase our property value by doing the things I am going to discuss in this little book.

So open your mind and get ready to possibly increase the property values in your community.

Are you ready? Lets do this!

Chapter 1

HOMEOWNER PRIDE IS APPEARANCE

ave you ever noticed a house that looks run down on the outside? The gutters have fallen down, it needs paint or the siding is coming off, the windows are old and out dated? You see an old broken down storage shed on the property filled with junk. And then to top it off you see a bran new Mercedes or BMW sitting on the drive way! What?

When you see a property that has old out of date windows, the siding is falling off or the gutters have fallen off the property looks almost abandon it looks terrible. When a realtor comes into your neighborhood to sell your house and the houses on your street look run down, then right there in the buyers mind, the property is not worth that much.

Just think about it for a minute. Would you pay top dollar for an old run down pair of shoes or an old torn up leather coat? NO!

So we as blacks have to start to keep up our homeowner pride by making sure our home looks great on the outside. The first impression a person gets of your home is how it looks on the outside. The outside of your house makes a lasting impression and affects value of your home and other homes in your community too.

I have been in some communities that the houses are painted in colors that aren't appealing to the public like bright red, lime green, dark purple etc... What? Yes it is your house and you own it but you must remember you are living in community it's not just about what you like because your decisions affect the entire community around you. It would be very difficult to sell your house if your neighbor house was painted dark purple with lime green accents!

So here is what you should do. Make sure your house is painted in a flattering neutral color. If you have siding make sure the siding is a flattering neutral color. Upgrade your windows, get rid of the old junk shed in the back yard. Get someone to your house to hang your storm gutters properly. Did you know that if your storm gutters are broken down when it rains your house can sustain water damage? And also did you know that in some cases your homeowner's insurance can help you pay for damage that has been done to your house. Some people believe that if you file a claim with your homeowner's insurance that your rate insurance will go up. But it has been my experience that this does not happen in most cases. That is what homeowner's insurance is there for. You pay it monthly so use it.

Chapter 2

CURB APPEAL

Oh I have so much to say about curb appeal! My favorite topic! Ok your grass should be green in the summer months. You say it is green. No I mean really green. I see so many people who don't want to water their lawns because they think it will make their water bills go up. Yes it will make it go up but it's worth it. Your property value and community is at stake here. So what your water bill will go up that is something you should budget for when you are a homeowner.

Secondly we as black people really have to work on the weed problem. First of all if you don't know that dandelions are considered weeds in your front lawn then you have a serious problem. You need to read up on how to care for your lawn. And if you don't want to read up on lawn care then hire someone to come and care and cut your lawn on a regular basis. Just think about it for a minute. A realtor comes to your community to sell your house and your neighbor's grass is full of weeds and big brown patches of dead grass in the lawn because they haven't watered it because they call themselves saving money. Well saving a little money on the water bill is costing you and your neighbors a lot of money, because you are not going to be able to sell your house at a higher price if your neighbors curb appeal is not attractive. You get it! What affects one affects the all in a community. We talk all this community stuff but we need to put it into action.

JOAN MARIE

Just having a newer car on the drive way is not considered curb appeal. So many times we as blacks think the newer car is all we need to show everyone that we are doing well as homeowners. But in reality having a newer car or even a brand new car will not increase the value of our homes in our communities. Having brand new sneakers and clothes won't increase the value of our homes. Hair and nails won't increase the value of our homes. You hear me?! You feel me?! Got it! Lol

So you need to get off your fanny and make sure that your home has beautiful green cut grass you might even want to plant some flowers and some colorful trees. Many of the black neighborhoods I have been in really don't have many trees. You know why? Well I have been told because trees drop the leaves and we don't like raking the leaves up. WOW! What?

Well let me tell you this, did you know that properties on a tree lined street are more valuable than properties on a street without any trees!

If you cut a tree down then you need to plant and grow another in its place. Trees and gardens in a community really make a community look beautiful. People are attracted to beautiful landscapes, flowers and trees. And, yes, it is good for the local wildlife too. Like I said before it's not just about you it's also about the community. We are truly ONE! Cut your grass, plant some flowers, get rid of the weeds and water your lawn.

Chapter 3

INTERIOR TALK

*N*ow let's go on the inside of the house and talk about what you can do to make it more valuable. The appearance of your interior walls is very important. If your interior walls are damaged with scuff marks or actual holes in them that will definitely decrease the value of your home. Make sure that your interior walls are painted in a warm neutral color especially when putting your house up for sale. And please make sure that you take that old paneling off the walls if you have it up. Many times when purchasing a home you will see paneling and if so make sure to ask the real estate person to a look behind the paneling. Sometimes paneling on the interior could be hiding wall damage, so be careful.

Your interior floors are very important. If you purchased the house with carpeting you will want to know how old the carpet is. If it is 10 years old you might really want to consider getting rid of it when you move in. Or if the carpet is fairly new but not a neutral color you might also want to get rid of it especially if you think you might be selling your property. Floors that are in good shape and with a nice neutral color carpet or wood floors can definitely increase the value of your property. Cha-Ching!

Your kitchen is extremely important and really affects the value of your house. Make sure that you have an updated appliance package, nice counter space and cabinets. If you purchased the house with an outdated kitchen, then it is imperative that you update the kitchen as soon as possible. Kitchens can increase the value of your home or decrease the value of your home.

Make sure that your bathrooms have been updated. I have seen so many homes that were built in the 60's with the original bathrooms! If you have purchased a home with outdated bathrooms it is extremely important to have them updated as soon as possible.

Remember that you might at some point want to take some equity out of your house for personal reasons so if you keep your house updated and in good shape it will benefit you financially while you are still living in it and also if you sell it.

Chapter 4

LOITERING

We need to stop our children from loitering in our neighborhoods. When I ride through other neighborhoods I don't see groups of teens walking through their streets. I only see this kind of behavior in our neighborhoods. This type of behavior actually makes the neighborhood appear to be unsafe.

Whenever I show a house in a black neighborhood, I see a group of young black males hanging around either at the playground or just on a corner. We need to tell our children to hang in the back yard. We need to tell our youth that hanging out on corners is very unsafe for our black males. With the police problems that are occurring all over the country with our young black men, we need to educate them to prevent as much as we can.

Many of us are not into prevention. I like to call us "firemen" because we wait until the problem happens and then we try to put the fire out. We as blacks need to practice prevention as much as we can. And if we can teach our young men to stay off the corners and out of the streets, this will prevent a lot of bad situations from happening.

Even if we have stores in our communities, you will see packs of young men hanging out in front of the stores. This will make it very difficult to have well-known stores in our areas. The loitering and robberies make our neighborhoods less likely to have nice stores in our communities. So if we get control over our children, we could stop our children from getting in trouble with law enforcement and we could also prevent all those no name stores from popping up in our communities. Now don't get me wrong: I like the idea of mom and pop shops, but those mom and pop shops should be black-owned. Don't you think so? Of course there will be other stores in our communities that are from different ethnic groups, which is acceptable. However, I feel that most of the stores should be black-owned.

Chapter 5

PAYING THE BILLS

I know that many of us can't pay our bills because of our employment situations however, I also know for a fact that many of us have our priorities wrong. We might have the money to pay an electric bill but decide to buy a new pair of shoes with it instead because we think that we have time to pay before they shut the lights off. This kind of thinking leads us to having our utilities shut off way more than they should be.

I realize that our unemployment rate is at an all time high, which causes many of our financial problems. However in many cases we just make poor decisions when it comes to budgeting our money. For example, many black people will purchase very expensive gifts during the holiday seasons only to find themselves in financial difficulty at the beginning of a new year. We must get and keep our priorities in focus no matter what the circumstances are.

Remember keeping your lights and gas on is very important especially if you have children. And many times our utilities are cut off not because we didn't have the money but because we made poor decisions with our money when we had it.

When we become homeowners, it is important to pay your house bills first. Pay your property taxes, your utilities and mortgage insurance. That is very important! Paying your property taxes helps pay for the school system in your communities. Paying your utilities keeps you warm in the winter and cool in the summer and also helps prevent fires. Many people that don't have electric or heat may tend to burn candles for light and use propane to provide heat. As a result of using candles and propane heaters many fires have been started in our communities. I know what I am talking about. I live in a predominately black community and see these types of fires all too often.

That brings be to just some basic stuff you should have in your house to prevent death or injury from a fire. Make sure you install fire alarms and carbon monoxide detectors in your home. They are both very inexpensive but really help a lot. Having both installed can save your life.

Chapter 6

MAKING GROWN-UP DECISIONS

I think we need to start making grown-up decisions when we become homeowners. Remember purchasing a home is a huge investment. It is much more important than purchasing a car. So we need to grow up. When you purchase a house you need to know that you must upgrade your home. For example, at some point you will have to paint the inside and outside of your home or put new siding up and a new roof. You will need to upgrade your washer and dryer – even if it still works – because if you have a 15-year-old washer and dryer, it is no longer energy efficient. If you have an old stove you need to upgrade it. If you have the same carpet on your floors for over 10 years, you should have new carpet installed. If you have old, single-pane windows, they should be replaced.

I know people that have never painted the outside of their house or had siding put on their homes and they have been in their homes for more than 10 years. Do you know that painting your home a nice neutral color will help protect the siding on your home? Did you know that if you replace that old siding with vinyl siding it will improve the value of your home and the appearance of your home? So if you can't afford vinyl make sure you paint your home. But if you can afford vinyl siding by all means get it because it will be well worth it!

New windows are very important for your home. Not only because it just looks better, but because they are more energy efficient. Having newer windows can save you on heating bills in the winter and electric bills in the summer when you run your air condition.

Upgrading your heating systems and air conditioning systems is very important. If you purchase a house and the systems are already 10 years old you might want to really think of having them replaced soon after you close. Did you know that some utility companies will allow you to have a new heating system or air condition installed and bill you monthly on your utility bill? Also if you have just purchased your home, your credit rating was good so you can also contact a installation company and have them install a new heating system/air conditioning system on credit. It will be worth your time and a good step to take to prevent your heating or air conditioning system breaking down in the winter or summer months.

Let's talk about your washer, dryer, dishwasher, stove and refrigerator. You definitely need to upgrade if they are over 10 to 15 years old. Upgrading your appliances will definitely increase the value of your home when you are ready to sell it. But it will also save your some money with your utility bills.

Many of us operate on the theory of "if it ain't broke don't fix it". Well when you are a homeowner you don't need to wait until the thing breaks before you replace it. Having old washer and dryers, refrigerators and stoves is not financially beneficial to you in any way. Just because a washer or stove is still working doesn't mean it doesn't need to be replaced.

Yes I know being a homeowner is a lot of responsibility. But it is a responsibility that helps our communities if we take it seriously and do what is needed to help increase the values of our homes. You see we do have the power we just have to start using it.

Chapter 7

PARTICIPATION IN COMMUNITY GOVERNMENT

re you involved in the community government? It is very important as a homeowner to be involved to some degree in the local government. Do you know that homeowners count? Homeowners have a lot of power in their communities because they are the ones that pay taxes! You should show up to your community meetings sometimes and read your community newsletters. You should call your municipal offices if you have any complaints. If a neighbor has gotten out of control and has trash all around their property you should put in a complaint. If you see a property really looking rundown, call your county/township or city offices and demand that someone comes out and takes care of the situation.

If you think that a property is abandoned and there may be squatters on the property, call the county offices. Remember that the community you live in has a direct affect on your property and the value of it.

Read up on the people running for office in your community. Get a chance to attend a meeting to hear them speak. It is very important that you also participate in local voting. As a homeowner and tax payer, you pay these people's salaries. So be a boss who keeps in touch with the local government in your area.

Chapter 8

YOUR LOCAL SCHOOLS

Ok now let's talk about why black parents are just not involved in the public school system. I know there are many reasons or excuses but if your child goes to public school you need to attend the parent teacher meetings. If you are a homeowner, you pay a tax that goes directly to the public school system.

I have so many friends who send their children to a private or catholic school that they pay for and they also pay their taxes for the public school system. That means you are paying twice. Now on average, black people make a lot less so, do we really have all this extra money to pay for school twice?

The public school system is truly a problem in predominantly black communities and here too we can vote them in or out. We have the power to elect people on a local level who will benefit us and our communities.

So all I can really say here is we need to get involved with our public school systems even if your children attend to private school because you are paying for the public schools in your communities if you are a homeowner.

TIPS WHEN PURCHASING A HOME

When you purchase a home here are some of the things you should be looking at.

Heating and Air-conditioning Systems

When you purchase a home you should have the heating and air-conditioning systems inspected. Make sure you ask the real estate sales person how old the heating system is. If the system is 20 years or older you may want to see if the sellers could replace it before you purchase the house. Your real-estate sales person will actually negotiate this for you.

The Roof

Make sure that you have the roof of the property inspected also. Ask the realtor how old the roof is as they are usually under warranty for about 20-25 years. You will want to see the paperwork to confirm that the roof has been inspected.

Electrical Systems

See to it that the electrical system is updated and in good working condition. You will definitely want the electrical system checked out by a home inspector.

Siding

When your realtor shows you a house, be sure to check out the siding. Make sure it is in good shape. Take a look around the entire outside of the house and if you see siding falling off or damaged make sure to point this out. It may be possible to negotiate a lower price with the seller or have them do repairs before you move in.

Windows

Make sure you look closely at the windows. They should be dou-ble-pane windows. If they are single-pane, you might want to see if the seller is willing to replace them. Again you can do this with the help of your realtor. Updating your windows will help you with the heating bills in the winter and electric bills in the summer.

Appliances

Did you know that having an updated appliance package can actually increase the value of your house? So if you are shown a house with an outdated appliance package, such as an old stove, refrigerator, dishwasher or microwave, you could ask that the price of the house be lowered. Or you could ask your realtor to talk to the seller to see if they are willing to upgrade the appliances. You will never know until you try.

Flooring

If the house you are going to purchase has carpeting you might want to have an housing inspector check it out for you. You don't want an issue that could be costly in the future to be covered up by carpeting so just make sure that you hire a housing inspector. Matter of fact, I would ask my realtor to refer a housing inspector.

Financing

Please make sure that when you do start looking for a home, that you can truly afford it. Never allow the realtor or anyone to convince you to purchase a home you cannot afford or that you can't pay for comfortably. Many times we are just hoping we can get approved for the mortgage and will agree to terms that we know we really can't afford. Stay within what you can afford and never allow anyone to convince you to purchase something beyond your means.

Air Duct Systems

It is very important to have the air duct systems cleaned either upon moving into a house or have the sellers clean the duct system before they move out. Many times people neglect to have their duct systems cleaned and sanitized which ca lead to unclean air flow in your home. If you have children or yourself suffer from allergies it is always important to have your duct systems cleaned and sanitized.

Author's Final Thoughts

I am hoping that this information will help you in your endeavors of being a homeowner. Being a homeowner is a positive thing. Owning property can be very powerful. You can leave your property to your children so that they won't have to start off in life with nothing. Owning property is very exciting and satisfying. When you can walk into your own home it just gives you a sense of satisfaction.

Being a homeowner gives you a sense of belonging to a community. We as blacks need to get more involved in our communities as home-owners. We pay taxes and therefore we are entitled to the programs and services that are available in our own communities.

Be proud of your community and take care of it. You might even want to plant a tree or start a community garden. Remember it is your community, so help make it the best it can be! And if we all do our part in our communities, it is my opinion that property values in black communities will increase much faster. It really is up to us.